The Cat That Grew and Grew

Level 8 – Purple

Helpful Hints for Reading at Home

The graphemes (written letters) and phonemes (units of sound) used throughout this series are aligned with Letters and Sounds. This offers a consistent approach to learning whether reading at home or in the classroom.

HERE IS A LIST OF PHONEMES FOR THIS PHASE OF LEARNING. AN EXAMPLE OF THE PRONUNCIATION CAN BE FOUND IN BRACKETS.

Phase 5			
ay (day)	ou (out)	ie (tie)	ea (eat)
oy (boy)	ir (girl)	ue (blue)	aw (saw)
wh (when)	ph (photo)	ew (new)	oe (toe)
au (Paul)	a_e (make)	e_e (these)	i_e (like)
o_e (home)	u_e (rule)		

Phase 5 Alternative Pronunciations of Graphemes			
a (hat, what)	e (bed, she)	i (fin, find)	o (hot, so, other)
u (but, unit)	c (cat, cent)	g (got, giant)	ow (cow, blow)
ie (tied, field)	ea (eat, bread)	er (farmer, herb)	ch (chin, school, chef)
y (yes, by, very)	ou (out, shoulder, could, you)		

HERE ARE SOME WORDS WHICH YOUR CHILD MAY FIND TRICKY.

Phase 5 Tricky Words			
oh	their	people	Mr
Mrs	looked	called	asked
could			

TOP TIPS FOR HELPING YOUR CHILD TO READ:

- Allow children time to break down unfamiliar words into units of sound and then encourage children to string these sounds together to create the word.

- Encourage your child to point out any focus phonics when they are used.

- Read through the book more than once to grow confidence.

- Ask simple questions about the text to assess understanding.

- Encourage children to use illustrations as prompts.

This book focuses on the grapheme /ou/ and is a purple level 8 book band.

The Cat That Grew and Grew

Written by
Robin Twiddy

Illustrated by
Angela Mayers

This is the story of the cat that grew and grew or, more importantly, the story of how I came to rule the Earth! That's me, Doug, the kid on the cat.

It all started with a Christmas present. I always wanted a cat, but there was no way to tell back then that I was about to get the best cat ever!

I called the cat Fred. Fred was the smallest cat I had ever seen. We were always together. Fred liked to sit on my shoulder when we went out.

After a week, Fred was too big to sit on my shoulder. It seemed odd that he had got so big so quickly. He seemed to be growing bigger by the second.

One evening, over soup, I asked Mum how she found Fred. She said that she found him the night the big comet from outer space crashed in old Billy's field.

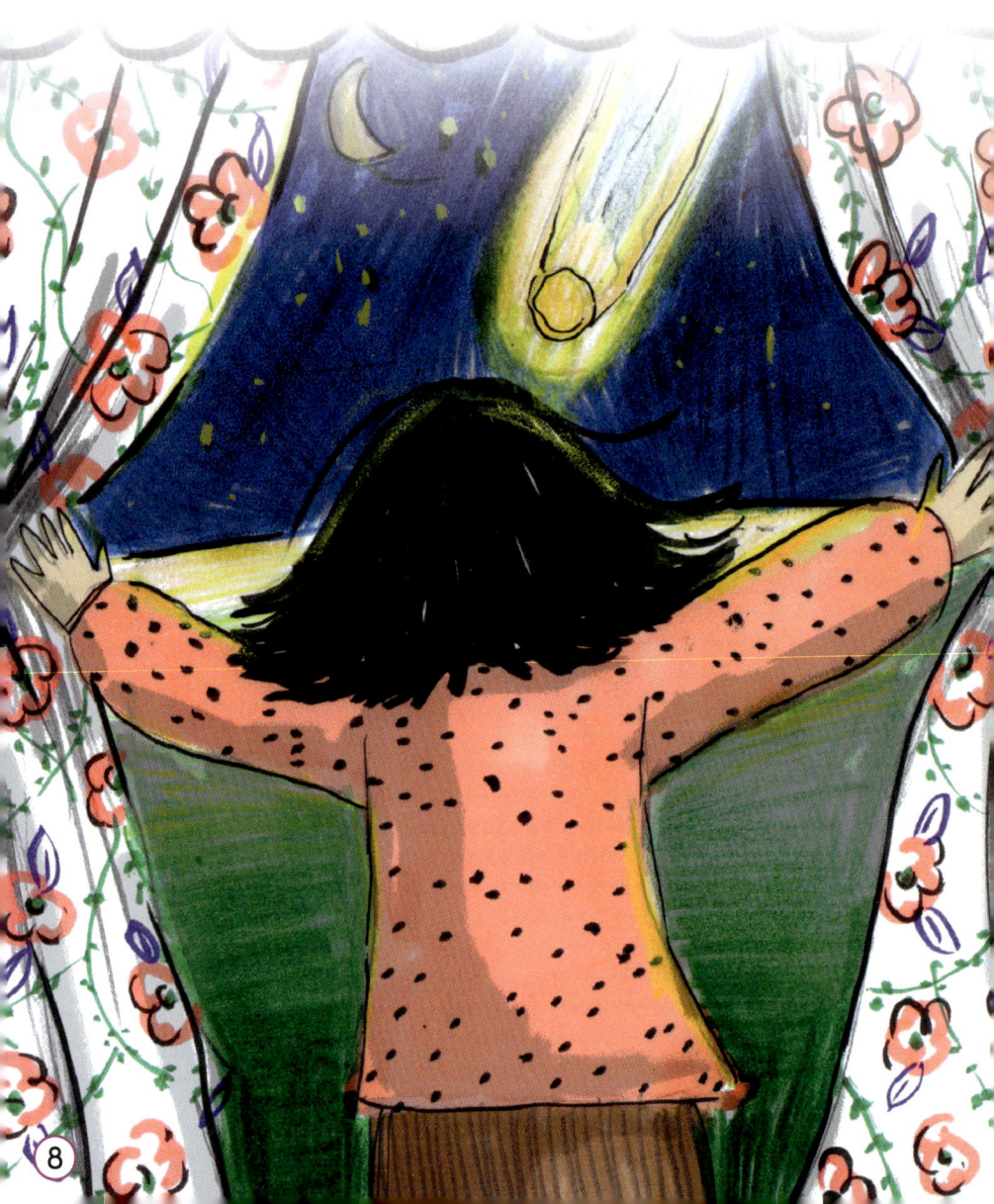

I began to wonder about Fred, was he a cat from outer space? Was he changed by the comet? Whatever the truth was, Fred was my best buddy.

The next morning Fred, jumped up onto my bed. The legs gave way with a loud snap. I bounced off the mattress and landed with a thud. Fred was as big as me now.

I could not wait to take Fred out to show him off to the other kids in town.
It was a nice summer day, without a cloud above us. We did get some strange looks.

I turned the corner into the alley beside the cinema, when I was suddenly pushed against the wall. It was Tim Short – the local bully. "Give me your pocket money!" he shouted in my face.

"Hey, why are you smiling?" asked Tim.
It wouldn't be long before he found out.
Silently, Fred crept around the corner and
pounced. Tim was pinned to the ground like
a mouse.

Tim never bullied anyone ever again. I told him that if he did, he would get another visit from Fred. Tim is now very kind to strangers and stray cats.

It was a few weeks after the Tim incident and Fred had grown even bigger. Fred had grown so large that I could mount him like a small horse.

Fred was running along the streets with me on his back when we found ourselves outside the council hall. Something was happening. A crowd was gathered outside, and they held up signs.

The head of the town council was shouting something about trousers at the crowd. I rode my cat up to one of the protestors.
"What's all this about?" I asked.

"He's trying to ban trousers," said the man.
"Why?" I asked.
"Because then we would have to pay for his shorts," said another man.
"Get them!" shouted the man in shorts.

The big men in shorts charged at the protesters. Without thinking, I dug my heels into Fred's flanks, and we pounced between the charging men in shorts and the protesters.

The air filled with whipping paws, and men in shorts found themselves thrown into fountains, flowerbeds and bins. The men understood that they were not a match for Fred.

I looked the man in shorts in the eye.
I explained that he needed to be nicer to
people and that he could not ban trousers.
He explained that he never wanted to meet
Fred again.

Fred grew even bigger. Soon, the papers found out about us, and we were famous. But being famous was not as good as I expected.
The prime minister had put a bounty out on us.

The army surrounded and attacked Fred. Missiles rebounded off his fur as if it was armour. A giant cat with a mouthful of tank took the fight out of them with ease.

The army surrendered, and the Queen made me the King of England. I kept the prime minister around but told him that he needed to be nicer to the people of England.

Over the next few weeks, Fred kept growing. By the time he was one year old, he looked more like a furry mountain than a cat. England was running smoother than ever under my rule.

I realised what I needed to do. That was when me and Fred started out on our tour of the Earth. We visited every leader of every country and had a chat with them.

Many of Earth's leaders were quick to hand over their crowns to me. I left the rulers in charge to run the countries but made it clear that if their people were not happy, Fred would be back.

Other leaders were not as quick to understand. They needed a little more of a push. Fred took care of that. Eventually, all of Earth's leaders had handed over control to me and Fred.

That is how I came to rule the Earth. Now, kids all over the planet eat ice cream when they like, and all the adults have to be nice to each other... or else.

The Cat That Grew and Grew

1. What was the bully's name?

   (a) Kevin Tall

   (b) Billy Young

   (c) Tim Short

2. If you could choose any pet to grow and grow like Doug's cat Fred, what would it be?

3. Where did Doug think Fred the cat might have come from?

4. What did Fred break by jumping on it?

5. Do you think Doug did the right thing becoming the ruler of the Earth?

© 2022 **BookLife Publishing Ltd.**
King's Lynn, Norfolk PE30 4LS, UK

ISBN 978-1-80155-478-7

All rights reserved. Printed in Poland.
A catalogue record for this book is available from the British Library.

The Cat That Grew and Grew
Written by Robin Twiddy
Illustrated by Angela Mayers

An Introduction to BookLife Readers…

Our Readers have been specifically created in line with the London Institute of Education's approach to book banding and are phonetically decodable and ordered to support each phase of the Letters and Sounds document.

Each book has been created to provide the best possible reading and learning experience. Our aim is to share our love of books with children, providing both emerging readers and prolific page-turners with beautiful books that are guaranteed to provoke interest and learning, regardless of ability.

BOOK BAND GRADED using the Institute of Education's approach to levelling.

PHONETICALLY DECODABLE supporting each phase of Letters and Sounds.

EXERCISES AND QUESTIONS to offer reinforcement and to ascertain comprehension.

BEAUTIFULLY ILLUSTRATED to inspire and provoke engagement, providing a variety of styles for the reader to enjoy whilst reading through the series.

AUTHOR INSIGHT: ROBIN TWIDDY

Robin Twiddy is one of BookLife Publishing's most creative and prolific editorial talents, who imbues all his copy with a sense of adventure and energy. Robin's Cambridge-based first class honours degree in psychosocial studies offers a unique viewpoint on factual information and allows him to relay information in a manner that readers of any age are guaranteed to retain. He also holds a certificate in Teaching in the Lifelong Sector, and a postgraduate certificate in Consumer Psychology.

Robin specialises in conceptual, role-playing narratives which promote interaction with the reader and inspire even the most reluctant of readers to fully engage with his books.

PHASE 5 /ou/
This book focuses on the grapheme /ou/ and is a purple level 8 book band.